Dear Single Woman

Messages of Inspiration and Self Love

About the Author

Dear Single Woman,

Usually this part is written from a third person point of view, but I am breaking protocol and talking to you personally. I am a Life Coach, Mentor, and Author. **Having** been in and out of the dating scene for over twenty years, I have worked with clients in regards to relationships of all kinds. While I am not a doctor or therapist, I am a **single woman** with lots to share. The most important relationship of my life, and the one that has taken the most work, has been the one with myself.

Love,
Me

Copyright © 2020 J. Day All rights reserved.

A catalogue record for this book is available from the United States library.

ISBN

All rights reserved. No part of this book shall be reproduced or transmitted in any form or by any means: graphic electronic or mechanical, including photocopying, recording, or by any information storage and retrieval system without written permission of the publisher except where permitted by law. Published by Indigo Papillon Publications,

Printed in United States

Acknowledgment
Cover art and design By J. Day

The information in this book is not for diagnosis, treatment, prescription of any physical/mental health disorders. This is also not a substitute for competent and licensed healthcare or financial professionals. Although every precaution has been taken in the preparation of this book, the publisher and author assume no responsibility for errors or omissions. Neither is any liability assumed for damages resulting from the use or misuse of the information contained.

Indigo Papillon Publications
Mailing Address Only
957 Rt. 33 Suite12
#337
Hamilton Square, NJ 08690

Dear Single Woman

Messages of Inspiration and Self Love

Special Thanks

A special thank you to my editors A.D. and K.L., without your encouragement, love and honesty, this book would not have been possible.

Dedication

This is dedicated to the women in my life who have supported me, uplifted me, and have been my tribe. You know who you are, and you are forever in my heart. Thank you for everything.

Table of Contents

Preface	8
Dating	9
Practical Matters	33
Family, Friends, or Foes	72
Lifestyle	86
Self-Love	113

Preface

As you may have already figured out, this is a book of letters, letters from me to you. In these pages, I will talk about relationships of all kinds: significant others, family, friends, and coworkers. There will be many topics covered, because sometimes when you navigate this world on your own; it is good to get some outside perspective. These are letters I would have written to my younger or future self, my friends, my family, or to my clients.

There is no one way or right way to live life, and it is not my objective to tell anyone what to do. My hope is that you can connect with these words as one woman to another. It is so important to know that your life can be incredibly fulfilling and happy while being single. There are many reasons why you may be single, and those reasons do not matter here. What matters is that you know that you are a bright, beautiful, and strong woman able to make a life for yourself, one that brings you joy.

You can read this book in order of letters or a few at a time for daily inspiration. I am including an index of first lines to help you find the topic or letter that speaks to you. The Kindle version will have a link to every tenth page in the index for easier navigation.

Enjoy, inspire and be your amazing self!

Dating

Dear Single Woman,

Do not waste time with someone who does not love you. This could be a friend, family member or significant other. You will often find that these relationships leave you exhausted and burnt-out. They are usually full of drama, games and tit for tat. Is that really what you are looking for? Are you looking for drama or someone to keep you walking on eggshells? It is possible that these types of relationships are comfortable, because they are what you are used to? If that is the case, you may want to begin to remove the old program: that drama and excitement is just not equal to love. The adrenaline of the emotional roller coaster can absolutely become your default, especially if you were raised in that type of drama-filled relationship structure. You have a choice though; you can choose surround yourself with people who bring you peace, stability and yes love.

Anyone who leaves you guessing loves themselves and the thrill of the game. This is a major rush for them; they are trying to boost their ego with your worry. It is selfish and manipulative. No one in your life should be allowed to treat you that way. People who really love you, will never leave you guessing; they will tell you how they feel and make you feel loved.

Love,
Me

Dear Single Woman,

If you do not want someone who plays games when dating, then stop playing them yourself. Be honest about who you are and what you want. Honesty is scary. It leaves you vulnerable and open to the pain that their truth may not be a match to yours. I have seen too many women and men complain that those they are dating hide things from them. They will not call for long stretches of time, and/or flirt with other people in front of their dates. They will say they want marriage or not, just to hook you. Then, they will suddenly act as if that was never the case. I could give tons of examples, but we must move on.

Get rid of the B.S.! Tell them how you feel: good or bad, and then honor their honest reaction. If they cannot be honest in return, it may be time to find someone who can. If you feel like your authenticity will not be well received, then why are you with them? Playing games are a sign of insecurity and immaturity. I get that a little mystery is fun and tantalizing, but you reach a point when you want something more, deeper. Even if it is not leading to a commitment, it's nice to know who you are dealing with.

Love,
Me

Dear Single Woman,

Stop with the emotional manipulation. Any person, who gives into that, has major self-esteem issues, and that is a problem you can't help them with. Moreover, if you're using that technique, ask yourself; why are you afraid of the word no? Love, real love respects a person's boundaries and feelings. Crying or using your emotions to change a person's response, will leave you wondering if they can ever really trust you with their heart. It is like asking someone for a gift; it ends up becoming a meaningless token. While gifts are great, if they are not coming from the heart, why would you want it? Someone who does what you want simply because you backed them into an emotional corner, isn't really in love with you, they are afraid of you. Maybe they love you and are doing what you say, because they do not want to lose you. That is inauthentic, and it will not lead to anything of real value.

Love,
Me

Dear Single Woman,

Dating can be fun, exciting and an adventure. Do not take it so seriously. So many people treat it as if it is their job or quest to find someone. The dates become interviews and completely suck the joy out of them. I understand not wanting to waste your time with someone who is obviously not right, but nowadays with online dating, you can have all of those answers before you even meet.

Remember that even the bad dates will have good qualities to take with you, like lessons, stories, and interesting memories. Enjoy the moments and just have fun. While you may not be on your dream date with the dream person, you will be doing something just as valuable, finding who and what you really want.

Love,
Me

Dear Single Woman,

Important dating lessons: Trust your instinct about a person. If they raise a red flag, do not ignore it. Let them pay if they want to, but carry cash just in case. First dates should never be at a movie, you just could not talk. Tell someone where you will be, always. Don't take out your cell phone unless you want to give the message, "I'm not into you." Do not trust someone who is rude to the wait staff or leaves a crappy tip. They will eventually be rude to you, too. Watch how they treat others who are close to them. How do they treat you around their friends or family? If it is poorly, that will not change later.

Love,
Me

Dear Single Woman,

How to read an online dating profile part 1:

- Stay away from pictures with a person cut out. If they cannot take the time to have a friend snap a good picture, or cannot manage a good selfie, then they just want a hookup.

- Does their profile have pictures with cars or boats? Then they are trying to bait you with money; they are not looking for someone with substance. If you took the bait, then you do not care if someone genuinely wants to know who you are and what is in that beautiful mind of yours.

- Be careful of the person whose picture includes their child or children (sometimes, included as bait). If they are this careless with their children's safety (freely posting their pictures), they may also be careless with yours. Let's not dismiss the fact that they may be looking for a free babysitter and/or just a hookup. You should not be meeting the children until the relationship is stable; it is extremely unfair to the kids.

Love,
Me

Dear Single Woman,

How to read an online dating profile part 2:

- Profile descriptions that are too short, speak of someone who is not serious about dating, or they have nothing to say about themselves. You deserve someone who knows themselves and what they want.

- On the flipside, stay away from the profiles that are very long, full of fluff and no substance. This can speak to insecurity or insincerity.

    Remember, a well thought out profile is just long enough to show some personality, but leave you a little intrigued. The tone should be positive and that of someone who is excited to get out there and find some romance, not just a hookup. If you are looking for a simple hookup, that is great, but both parties need to be honest about what they are expecting.

Love,
Me

Dear Single Woman,

When going out on a date, it is ok to allow someone to pay. You can treat them next time or cook something nice on the next date. You do not owe them anything. If someone treats you to a meal, movie, drinks, or any other date activities, it should be because they like you and enjoy treating you to something special. It should never be, because they think that you will "put out." Just in case, always have a card or some cash with you. This way if they decide to use what they "gave" to you to get something physical, then you pay your share and get out of there

Love,
Me

Dear Single Woman,

So much knowledge exists within the void. Understanding comes when someone does not answer your question. When someone ignores you, listen to that, it is information. This does not mean that you fill in the blanks. They filled in those blanks already. That person no longer wants your company or that business is not interested in hiring you. Do not feel as if you have lost out or that they have. Do not feel as if you must change to meet their needs; rather find someone or some place that needs you as you are. If you want to change because your heart is telling you that you are ready for something different, go for it. Do not, however, go shaving your edges to fit a puzzle, or push yourself into a box that was never yours to begin with.
Love,
Me

Dear Single Woman,

Your significant other or anyone in your life should not make you feel insignificant. They should not put you down, give you the silent treatment, and threaten to withhold affection. That is not love; that is manipulation. While relationships can have their complications, love is rather simple. You want what is best for them. Their joy is your joy; their pain is your pain, etc. This goes for friends and family members. I am blessed with family and friends that both cry with me and root for me. My dating life was a sharp contrast; this is why I am currently single. When I find that one person to join my team, and I join theirs, I will know. It is old fashioned, but 1 Corinthians 13:4-7 put it very well:

Love is patient, love is kind. It does not envy, it does not boast, it is not proud. It does not dishonor others, it is not self-seeking, it is not easily angered, it keeps no record of wrongs. Love does not delight in evil but rejoices with the truth. It always protects, always trusts, always hopes, always perseveres.

It does not matter what your faith is, if you have any at all. Those are wise words, if you want a checklist for whom to keep around you. Will every great relationship check off the entire list all of the time? No, we are human, and we will make some slip ups. If we, and the people we surround ourselves with, are like this most of the time, then the bonds will have a chance to flourish.

Love,
Me

Dear Single Woman,

Sometimes people lie. They lie to themselves, and they lie to you. This is especially true when you are in the dating pool. I am not saying that they are all liars; it is just that so very many people have no idea what they want. They go into the date wanting one thing: marriage, kids, and deep connections, fill in the blank. In the end, they wanted something light, fun and with as little connection as possible. Many of them say that they do not want games, but end up playing them anyway. They say that they want someone who is emotional, until they actually see them get emotional. It is not completely their fault. We do not always know what we do not want until we have actually experienced it. Be honest about what you want and learn to read people's actions to see if they match their words.

Love,
Me

Dear Single Woman,

Stop dating potential and start dating realities. When you find yourself saying, "They are so nice to me. You just can't see it." Stop that. If no one else can see it but you, then the person you are dating is not really being very nice to you. "Oh they are just having a bad day." "They don't want kids now, but they might someday." or any other excuse for why they could be right for you down the road. NO, NO, NO. Stop excusing bad behavior or someone who have vastly different wants in life. If you want children and they say they do not, take it at face value. If they are not nice in public, but nice in private, that is not a great sign. Potential does not make a great relationship. Honestly, respect, and great communication can.

Love,
Me

Dear Single Woman,

When you are dating, and the two of you decide to take the big step into commitment, you are trying to find a path that you can both walk together. Even though you are walking the same path, it is critical to understand that you still each have your own journey to follow. Your partner should not be seen as the entirety of your life. The source of all that brings you joy. If you are looking for someone to solve all your problems and be perfect to boot, then you are setting both of you up for failure. You also have to ask yourself how you measure up as Ms. Perfect in the eyes of your partner. Neither should expect perfection; rather expect love, respect and communication. Go in with the knowledge that you will each grow and change, both as individuals and as a couple. Take delight in these changes and encourage each other. Remember, that as a team, you take on different roles to support a singular goal.

Love,
Me

Dear Single Woman,

The dating world can be exciting and exasperating. You envision the person you want to be with; some of you will create lists, vision boards, even entire books in your head of what this person will be. If you are consistently finding yourself in relationships or on dates with the exact opposite of what you want, then it is time for some self-reflection. Spend months, and yes, sometimes years getting to know yourself. Who are you? What do you need? What do you want out of life? Then give all of it to yourself. Do not wait for someone to fill that void, they cannot. Some will say, "If I do it myself, then what am I leaving for my partner to do?" That line of thinking will lead you to a constant state of feeling as if something is missing. What happens if it doesn't work out? Oops, it goes missing again. You end up feeling as if everyone you date is your soul mate, because of a temporary filling of that void. That is a lot of pressure to put onto one person. In addition, how are they supposed to know who you are and what will make you happy, if you have not figured it out yourself?

Love,
Me

Dear Single Woman,

As we touched on before, you must ask yourself the question, "who am I," before looking to bring someone else into your life. You are complex and yes, you have your entire life to figure it out, but do not wait until you are too miserable to begin the search. If you learn what makes you tick, then you can be honest right from the beginning and allow you both to make an educated decision about your feelings for one another. Do not try to be the person they want you to be and do not expect that from them. If you are a good match, great, if not, move on to find someone who is. Even if that means, you are your own perfect match.

Love,
Me

Dear Single Woman,

Let us touch again on the subject of whom it is that you are attracting, verses who it is you want. There is something called the Law of Attraction. Now, it may come under many names, but the nutshell is that if you are attracting toxic relationships repeatedly, then you may need to remove some toxic inner dialogue or actions. If you say, I want someone who gives me their time, but you work 80 hours a week or consistently give your free time to the needs of others, then you will attract someone who also never has time for you. If you want someone to tell you how beautiful you are, then stop telling yourself about all of your physical flaws. You want someone who is generous; you got it, start giving to yourself. You want someone who is active in the community, then get out there and get that energy in your life by involving yourself. You have to make sure that the words you tell yourself and the actions you take are a match to the person you are trying to attract to you.

Love,
Me

Dear Single Woman,

If you are looking to get married or have a long-term partner, make sure to find someone with similar interests as you. If you like to travel, find someone who also likes to travel. If you love to cook, it would be great to find someone to cook with or at least someone who likes to eat. While it is important to have your own interests and passions, you also do not want to spend your life waiting for the other person to be finished on whatever else it is that they are interested in. A few hours of alone time are great, but it is nice to be able to explore this world with someone too, as my grandmother says, "someone to ooh and aah with."

Love,
Me

Dear Single Woman,

Do not settle. You are better than settling and worth more than that. While this could refer to a job, a home, or relationship, I am speaking about relationships right now, to be more specific, a significant other. Most single people, at one point or another, want and crave to be part of a couple, but being in the wrong relationship is much worse than being single. You may find yourself in the wrong relationship. That is okay. Be strong enough to release it, wish them well, and move on without regret. You will find that your life is a lot happier and lighter on your own for a while.

Love,
Me

Dear Single Woman,

This is advice I got from my mother early on, "Don't be a doormat." The problem is, you may not always realize it when it is happening. You may be completely smitten and thinking that you are doing something nice for the one that you care about. Ask yourself if you are always making excuses, to yourself or others, for their behavior or lack of participation in the relationship. If you find that you are always the one doing the compromising, the changing or being talked down to, then you need to question the health of your relationship. In some cases, there is a fine line between being a doormat and being abused. This happens in all kinds of relationships, not just romantic ones. You can give them a chance to change, and if they do not; walk away. Be strong and remember there is a difference between being kind and being a doormat!

Love,
Me

Dear Single Woman,

Being single in your twenties is a fun and exciting adventure. It is filled with anticipation and more questions than answers. You are still trying to figure out who you are, and they are also trying to figure things out, as well. You may find that person that you want to start a life with, and you create a family (just the two of you or maybe babies (fur or human). Some of you will sail through your twenties, dating all of the wrong people, with a few good ones sprinkled in there somewhere. You will attend showers of all kinds as the people around you make these huge life choices. During all of this, you may feel pressure from family, friends, society, or yourself to just find someone and get on with your life. Please do not do that. Take your time, enjoy the good and bad dates alike, or focus on yourself and your career. You have the right to do that. Your twenties can be a time of incredible fun and joy. Do not rush it along to fit someone else's timeline.

Love,
Me

Dear Single Woman,

Oh the thirties, sweet, quirky thirties. You may or may not still be in the dating game. Girl, you have grown up! You are far more savvy! You have entered a more mature stage; the qualities you may have wanted in a partner, in your twenties, have evolved. You are slowly replacing your insecurities with the "got to get stuff done," attitude. By now, the idea of going on a date has lost some of its sparkle. Oh sure, flirting is still fun; who does not like to be noticed? However, you are tolerating less of the nonsense that you saw and put up with in your twenties. The emotional games have gotten a bit old and listening to one more person give you, what essentially amounts to, a resume on your 100th first date, seems ridiculous. Who has time for that? You are a woman on the move and good luck to anyone who can catch you!

Love,
Me

Dear Single Woman,

Here we are in our forties. A woman in her forties knows what she wants from life and what she wants in her relationship. Dating is less of a priority and taking care of herself, and those she cares about, becomes top on the to do list. Now some of you in your forties may not be there quite yet. You know what? Embrace it! Stop caring about what everyone else thinks of you and hold your head up high. Understand that you are a powerhouse; you are the goddesses that the ancients wrote about in texts. In ancient times, you would have been the counsel, the one everyone else looked to for wisdom. While civilization has changed, the status of the "forty and fabulous" has not changed. Remember, **YOU** pave the way!

Love,
Me

Dear Single Woman,

Welcome to your 50's! A woman in her fifties is strong, confident, and takes no prisoners! They can have highly active social lives, working on self-improvement and thriving in their careers. Some of them are even looking at their second career; re-inventing themselves. Their lives are full of so many of the same things that we expect to see of women who are in committed relationships. They volunteer, travel, and dote on the children in their circle of family and friends. Some prefer their alone time and get lost in their interests and hobbies. I remember being young and taught that to have a full life, I must be married and have children. This, so far, has not been the case. I have not shunned these things, I just have not settled for the wrong relationships. One status is no better than the other. There are pros and cons to both. Happiness or misery could be at the end of either path; it depends on attitude and choice. Instead of defining yourself by either of the terms taken or single, try using words like confident, independent, happy, strong, smart, creative, and/or powerful.

Love,
Me

Practical Matters

Dear Single Woman,

There is no hand strong enough to lead you into your perfect future. This, you must do for yourself. Your future is an evolving flow that can only be created and made by you and the steps you take. Take the time, before making your next move, so that you can look back on that moment with the satisfaction that you did the best that you could. Take joy in creating your future, by relishing the current moment. When you plant seeds in a garden, you can only control how you plant and nurture them as they grow. You cannot control the weather, the animals, or the quality of the seeds. Take care of what you can control, and trust that everything else is happening as it should.

Love,
Me

Dear Single Woman,

You are the perfection in your job. You do not need to wait for the perfect job to find you or sit and complain about the one you have. All it takes is a shift of the attitude. No matter what job you have or what career path you have chosen, there will always be a down side. You will have bosses and coworkers who drive you nuts or throw you under the bus. There will be the customers who are never satisfied and find fault with everything. That does not mean it is a horrible job, rather, shift your focus to the people who appreciate you. Be the light in the darkness of your workspace. Ask to start a praise wall, where you boost each other up. Be the one who brings in the surprise coffee or tea for your work peeps. Focus on the client who loves what you do, and ask for a testimonial. There are hundreds of ways to lighten up a bogged down environment, but adding to it with bitterness and anger, will only make you resent it more. I hate to say it, but you will never move up and out unless people are able to see you bring something to the table. Start with a great attitude and the rest will follow. If all else fails, be blessed by the paycheck and plan something fun for the end of your workweek!

Love,
Me

Dear Single Woman,

To the capable adults, the world owes you nothing. It does not owe you a job, home: nothing! You have the right to earn, work for or find these things. This may sound harsh, but once you set aside the idea that you need to control the world and the people around you into giving you what you feel you deserve, you can set about getting it for yourself. Every human has the right to have choices, and to be able to make them freely.

Your vibration is responsible for these things coming into and out of your life. Sometimes opportunity appears in front of us, and it is our job to take it or not. Sometimes life takes an unfortunate turn; it is our job to learn from it and make it better. You are very capable and strong.

Love,
Me

Dear Single Woman,

There is a theory that for a child to learn and grow developmentally, we must meet their basic need first. Adults are no different. If you find that your life feels disorganized and you are feeling scattered and/or distracted, you need to ground. Grounding is a twofold process: Center yourself mentally and physically. To center mentally, take a walk, vent, write a list stretch, meditate or do something creative. That is an abbreviated list. To ground physically: Get enough sleep so that your body may physically rest. Exercise to keep your body healthy and to burn off any excess emotions. Pay your bills on time. When your bills are paid and on time, both your physical and mental worlds will relax. Clean your living space. It is difficult to thrive when you are worried about your physical health and well-being. It may take time, but investing that time into your well-being will keep you more focused in all other areas of your life.

Love,
Me

Dear Single Woman,

Worry/fear never solved anything on its own. We are programmed to worry and to be afraid; it is what keeps us safe, it is what alerts us to danger, but the worry itself is only a warning system. Action and planning is ultimately, what takes us from fear to a place of security. If someone hands you a heavy stone and asks you to hold it, how long will you carry it before sitting it down? Often, worries are handed down from generation to generation, or friend to friend. Once you are aware of a worry or fear, stop and ask yourself a few simple questions:
Is it mine?
- If the answer is "No," Let it go.
- If yes, then ask: Is there anything I can do about this problem? If yes, then take some steps to solve it again. If it is "No," let it go and do something positive in another area of your life.

If you are still stressed, breathe in and breathe out, life is much better when you breathe.

Love,
Me

Dear Single Woman,

The world is full of opportunities, of moments and crossroads, where you must make a choice. You can choose to stay exactly who and where you are, or to take a chance and leap into a new version of your life. This leap is one of faith and not guaranteed, which is exactly what makes them so scary. It is okay to stay where you are and to stick with the path you are on already. Just know that when you do, you cannot complain that you never have any opportunities. Have fun and remember that not making a choice is choosing to stay stuck!

Love,
Me

Dear Single Woman,

Life is full of contrasts and those contrasts define each other. They amplify and sharpen our reactions to them. Enjoy the differences and learn to find peace in each one. I wish no one sorrow in their lives, but it is inevitable. We lose people, jobs, places, money and opportunities. We forget, when in the throws, that this is the natural course of life. It is usually painful, that is natural. When it does come, take time to register your feelings. Then, try to reflect on forgiving the situation, releasing with love and rejoice in what is yet to come. Remember that the sun is sweeter after the rain.

Love,
Me

Dear Single Woman,

Some clichés for you today: Money cannot buy you happiness, but it can bring some stability. Murphy's Law says that anything that can happen, will, and at the worst possible time. You might as well get a good laugh and story out of it. Keep your friends close and your enemies closer… this way you get all the gossip. Lying does not make your nose grow, but it will show up on your face. Just tell the truth. Always wear clean underwear; you never know what situation you may end up in by the end of your day. Lastly, put the book down and get some beauty sleep.

Love,
Me

Dear Single Woman,

Your life will have many highs and lows; this is a fact. If you take credit for the good times, you must also take credit for the bad. Remember that you bring both into your life for a reason, often for a bigger picture that you cannot yet see. Be patient, and allow time to work its magic. If you can find the patience, you will quickly move through the difficult times and really relish the good. Those low times, though, will leave you gems that you cannot find anywhere else.

Love,
Me

Dear Single Woman,

Do not get so caught up with work that you forget to live. Get in the habit of breaking your patterns; this will keep your passion for life fresh. Join new groups, travel to new places, take weekend classes, or try a new hobby. Life should be more than: Wake up, go to work, sleep, and repeat. Enjoy everything life has to offer.

Love,
Me

Dear Single Woman,

It is okay to be sad, angry, or disappointed. Feel your feelings and work through them. The trick is to be proactive. If you need help, get it. If you need to cry, go for it. Do not get trapped by those feelings, to the extent that you convince yourself there is no way out. The way out is to experience the full force of them, and then allow yourself to shift into a better place. Try to find the lessons or the bigger meaning(s) that will give purpose to something that, at the time, may feel senseless.

Love,
Me

Dear Single Woman,

Y.o.l.o. (You only live once) can be a poor excuse to do stupid things, or it can be the reason that you take the time to live your life well. Life is indeed a fleeting moment in the scheme of things, and if you are going to take chances or risks, make sure that it is something you really want. Take the risk of opening your own business, going to school, moving to a new place, or seeing the world. Do not reconnect with toxic people, or do things that will harm yourself or others. If you do things correctly, then you will not live once, but many times within the one you are living.

Love,
Me

Dear Single Woman,

I wish for you a life full of contrasts, ones that bring you a greater appreciation, not just of one side, but of both sides. We often crave a life that is smooth and peaceful. Eventually, you may find that you are bored. This boredom can lead to unwise choices, simply to give your life a bit of drama. Instead of moving in that direction, look for creative challenges. Try a new hobby, take on a new exercise routine, reorganize, or find a new group of friends with which to interact. There are so many ways to bring in contrast that will add joy to your life instead of creating drama, just for the sake of it.
On the flip side, if you feel as if life continues to deal you a bad hand, stop and try to find a positive. For example, a forest fire is devastating, but can lead to immense regrowth and a renewal of life in the affected area. A breakup, while painful, can lead to a new sense of self and freedom that brings in opportunities!

Love,
Me

Dear Single Woman,

Life can change in an instant, for better or worse. The change itself is often not what causes us difficulty; it is the suddenness and our inability to prepare. When these changes do happen in your life, stop and take stock of what is within your control. Take some immediate steps to reduce your stress level. This could be creating a revised life plan, taking stock of finances, or calling a friend or family member to talk over your feelings and perhaps get some more ideas or a new perspective. This is by no means a comprehensive list, just a few ways that you can regain a feeling of empowerment in an otherwise disempowering situation.

Love,
Me

Dear Single Woman,

There is an old saying that the only thing that never changes is change itself. You can rely on your world to change and often. It can always be for the better, even when you do not realize it at the time. These changes are doors opening for you. These are opportunities for you to stop and make a decision. These decisions can move you closer to happiness or father away. The trick is not worrying about the right decision, rather taking the time to feel yourself being pulled and guided by the light and wisdom within. I often tell my students/clients that you have everything you need within you already; you just need to ask the right questions. When your world gives you a sharp turn or jolt, take a moment and start asking questions. Why now? What am I going to have room for in my life now? What was taking my energy that should not have been? These questions will not only help you to turn a negative into a positive, but it will also help you to build trust in yourself again.

Love,
Me

Dear Single Woman,

Life is a river constantly moving us forward through time. We can turn our heads back to see where we have been, but the further downstream we move the fuzzier our past looks, until it becomes a memory of a memory. Do not glorify or demonize your past; it is almost never as beautiful or as bad as our memories make it out to be. It often lacks the perspective of those around you. Those people who made such lovely memories with you, also at one point hurt you, even in tiny ways. The opposite is true, some of the worst people in our lives brought to us something good, even if it was through the lens of a lesson. Those moments of struggle may have brought us bigger success, and those wins we had, often brought with it unforeseen repercussions. The trick of looking at our past is to keep everything in balance and love it for what it was. They were the building blocks that make us who we are now.

Love,
Me

Dear Single Woman,

It is important to live in both the big picture and the small. Each moment is an opportunity and a choice that will add a single thread to the tapestry of your life. These small beautiful moments will bear the responsibility of working with every other choice to create your personal big picture. The trick is to not become tangled in the minutiae of the small decisions, allowing the bigger picture to slip away. In the same way, an author has to maintain the plotline, while still developing all of the characters, motivations, scenery and the details of the world that they are creating. Keep it all in balance so that you will not feel the need to rewrite it later!

Love,
Me

Dear Single Woman,

There are times when backslides are important and can lead to bigger and better things later. Our lives are not lived with never ending momentum. Oh, they can be, but then you can burn out or miss some important lessons. Days of rest and feeling unmotivated can lead to huge transformative breakthroughs! Enjoy the blocks, pauses, and stalls. Sometimes that is where life happens!

Love,
Me

Dear Single Woman,

If you wake up dreading the beginning of your workweek, it is probably time for a change. It may not be a need to leave your job; it may require a shift of your attitude. Simple changes can alter your work life in big ways. Meditate during your lunch breaks, or go for a walk. If you can, personalize your space, and put up some motivational notes. Make fun plans for after work, so that you have something to look forward to. Avoid the negativity, and do not take it personally. There is always that choice to look for other jobs, and if possible, while you still have one. Do not look out of desperation. Instead, look because you are inspired. Do not look, because you are angry, but because you are ready for something better or more challenging. Whether you stay or go is far less relevant than the attitude and energy you bring to the table.

Love,
Me

Dear Single Woman,

Stay on top of your health. Get your vitamin levels checked regularly. Go for your mammograms, and do self-exams regularly. When something is off, talk to your doctor. Putting off these tests will not make the issues go away. Listen to your own body, learn to read your results, ask many questions and do not be afraid to do a little research. (Always ask your doctor about what you find out on your own.) Do not be afraid of what you will find by looking; instead take back your power, by caring for your body in every possible way!

Love,
Me

Dear Single Woman,

Pay attention to the songs that run through your mind. Often they speak to unconscious parts of ourselves. Not the tunes that you pick up because they are playing on the radio hundreds of times, rather the music you hear once and stays with you. Maybe you tear up or fill with joy when you hear it. Perhaps it makes you want to dance or express anger. Let the feelings sweep over you and lean into them. Look up the lyrics and see what stands out to you? Often a particular phrase or sentence will really jump out and have meaning for where we are in our lives. This is your subconscious giving you direction or hints as to what you need in your life. Once you figure it out, it can help you know where to throw your focus.

Love,
Me

Dear Single Woman,

Stress is a fact of life. Find a healthy way to deal with it, and inner peace will no longer be a dream, but an everyday occurrence. You cannot always control the root of your stress, but you absolutely can take steps to diffuse it. Here are some possibilities

Work stress:
1. Take frequent mind breaks and breathe differently for 5 minutes
2. Have a meditation track to listen to either during your work or on one of your breaks.
3. (Think deeper and slower).

Financial stress:
1. Make a budget and eliminate unnecessary expenses.
2. Renegotiate cable, insurance, memberships, etc...
3. Reassess any automatic withdrawals.

Relationships:
1. Take a break (time and space)
2. Speak your truth without attacking, shaming or guilting the other person.
3. Take time to enjoy each other's company on a regular basis and tell them, regularly, why you appreciate them; this will benefit you both.
4. Get counselling from a professional, spiritual leader, trusted advisor or loyal friend.

This is the very short list of steps you can take to bring about a sense of empowerment in different situations. However, music, dance, yoga, art and other such activities can also help with general stress. Take time for self-care and empowerment!

Love,
Me

Dear Single Woman,

Sometimes in life, you do not get the apple for the fruit, but for the seed. The fruit may provide immediate gratification, but it provides very little for your long term. If, however, you save the seed and plant them, you will have fruit for the rest of your life. Money is like that, too. Save and invest, even if it is in amounts as small as a seed. As soon as you begin working, start your retirement funds. When money is tight, save your change, when money is rolling increase your savings. Do not ignore the power of how pennies and nickels can add up. I once heard the story of a family who had very little money, but every member of this large family would save their spare change to contribute to the family pot. They would store it in jars, bottles and whatever containers they could find. Eventually, the family saved enough change to buy a house. The single drop of water, that drips repeatedly, can wear a hole in a stone. Life does not have to change in an instant, but many instances can change your life.

Love,
Me

Dear Single Woman,

Even on your laziest day, find one thing to cross off of your "to do" list. You will thank yourself for doing this when you finally set upon doing all of your tasks. The mountain you were dreading, is a little bit smaller and more manageable. The next day you will not look back with regret, but instead with pleasure. Then, you can look forward to the next one.

Love,
Me

Dear Single Woman,

Let the pain sting, and the anger wash over you. When you hide those feelings away, a future version of yourself will have to deal with them. The future self that thought they moved on, that thought that those emotions had already been processed and dealt with, will eventually face their inner truth. Do it now. Why put it all off? Rage on until there is nothing left but resignation and then you can work on forgiving whoever needs to be forgiven. Resignation has a better chance of turning into inner peace than repressed anger ever could.

Love,
Me

Dear Single Woman,

When you hit an obstacle in your life, learn to strategize and make a plan. It is fully empowering to take a situation that, at first, may cause anxiety and use your wit and knowledge to turn it to your benefit. The best plans are not rigid, rather flexible and allow for you to make adaptations as needed. There may, at first glance, feel as if your options are limited, but often with more time, creative thinking and patience, new openings appear. If you are driving and you come to a giant tree blocking the road, you may think that your only options are to wait until someone clears it for you or to turn back around. That is only if you absolutely must keep your car with you. You could try parking to the side and climbing over it, under it, around it and getting to your destination by foot. You could turn the car around and find an alternative route around on a completely new road. You could go back home, leave the car and start your journey again by train. There are so many options for one problem, but if we only focus on the problem, it can be impossible to see a solution.

Love,
Me

Dear Single Woman,

Opportunity does not knock once and when one door closes; you may have to stop looking at doors all together. I have found that lessons and chances repeat themselves until we make the change to get it right. Now, it may not be with the same person or the same job, but the chance to get yourself to the right place on your path will happen. Trust that you are where you are supposed to be and that if you do not like the choice you made, you will be presented with the chance for a redo. It may not be with the same exact person, place, or job, but with the same type of energy or lesson attached.

Love,
Me

Dear Single Woman,

Indecision can be absolutely crippling when it comes to making a move. I am all for weighing out the options, researching your head off, and asking around for a few wise opinions. In the end, you have to take a leap of faith and know that whatever decision you have come to, will be the best possible one you could have made. Do not let past missteps keep you from taking your next ones. We all fall and get back up; that is how we learn. Have a heart to heart with your inner self, your higher self and your future self about where you want this choice to take you. Once you have the best answer, go for it!

Love,
Me

Dear Single Woman,

Sometimes you cannot, "Just get over it." Some feelings and issues must take their time to settle and then diffuse. You will always have the people around you who are supportive, and you will always have the people who want to rush you to move on. The latter are just uncomfortable and do not know how to help, or they are dealing with their own heaviness. Do remember, though, that there is a difference between dealing with something and dwelling in it. Do not relive your trauma by bringing it back up on purpose. Yes, it may be triggered. That is different from what I am discussing.

I am referring to:
There you are, finally having a good time. Suddenly, you feel as if you do not deserve this good time, or that people (or you) have forgotten your pain, so you bring it up.

It is okay if you forget you were hurt; that is healing. Grief works like that. You can be desperately sad, emotionally aching for days to months on end, and then suddenly, something makes you smile or laugh. After a while, the joy spends more time in your soul than the sadness, until one day you are renewed.

Love,
Me

Dear Single Woman,

Winning is a state of mind. It depends on what you want as the outcome. If you teach a child how to play a game, you allow them to win, then you lose the game, seeing the joy on that child's face, ends up being the real win. That same child loses the next three games, because now you want them to gain skills and learn to problem solve. Those losses are now the real victory, because the child gained something important. It is perspective and mindset. You cannot win unless you know what it is you really desire. So figure it out before you play the game.

Love,
Me

Dear Single Woman,

There is no magic or luck involved in having a happy life. Living a happy life does not mean that every day is glorious, filled with rose gardens and never-ending abundance. It means that the person finds abundance everywhere. They see and find reasons to be filled with joy. They have learned the art of letting shit go. Yes, that's right I said it. You have to decide what is important in life and choose your battles wisely. If you are constantly angry over something or someone, perhaps it is time to ask why me? I do not usually advocate this question, as it stimulates the inner victim. Chances are you have already been asking the question, but with the subtext: "Why do bad things always happen to me?" "Flip it around and ask: "Why do I keep focusing on the bad things?" Similar question, but one places the responsibility of your happiness on external forces, while the other allows you to feel empowered and take responsibility for your own happiness.

Love,
Me

Dear Single Woman,

There are life skills that every person should know when living on their own, and I will talk about them over the next few letters. Let us begin with cooking. You do not have to be a chef, but this is a basic human need. Frozen fruits and veggies are your friends. They are fresh, pre- cut, quick and convenient. Add rice, and some sort of protein, and you have an easy meal. You can do plant-based protein; it does not matter. Get the basic tools with which to cook:

- A basic pot and pan set, something nontoxic like stainless steel.
- Pyrex bakeware in a few different sizes.
- Cooking utensil set
- A few decent knives (watch a tutorial on how to be safe)
- A good veggie peeler
- Measuring cups
- Measuring spoons
- Liquid measuring cup

I am sure that I may be missing a few items, but you do not need to go crazy buying these, and your loved ones may even have some extra lying around that they would be willing to give you!

Take the time to experience new foods and flavors. Play, eat, and enjoy!

Love,
Me

Dear Single Woman,

So cooking is only one life skill that you may need to use. Sewing is another. You do not need to throw out your favorite shirt or pants because a button fell off! For a few dollars, you can create or get a sewing kit. There are plenty of tutorials to help you, as well. Sewing machines are nice, but not necessary for the quick repairs. Taking your favorite jeans that can no longer be worn and turning them into a cute tote bag or throw pillow is easy. Repairing a little hole, can save you money and help you keep a well-loved item. Everyone was taught these skills by their parents, once upon a time. We now have such a throwaway society, that the skills have gotten lost, and we rely on wasteful behaviors. With patience and practice, you may discover that not only are you able to repair, but create something all your own.

Love,
Me

Dear Single Woman,

Living alone can lead to some delightful discoveries! There are skills that every adult should know and be prepared for:

- Snake a drain
- Plunge a toilet
- Changing the various filters around your house
- Testing your smoke detector
- Change a tire
- Balance a checkbook
- Simple sewing
- Pump your gas
- Know what the lights mean on your car dashboard

This is a very short list, but it gives to a good idea. This could be a fun night with your family, coming up with a list of what they think is important for a single adult to know. The list your Grandparents have will look quite different from the list your parents give you. What are some things you don't know how to do, but would like to?

Love,
Me

Dear Single Woman,

Living your life peacefully and being financially secure, requires learning how to create a budget. It takes time and monthly maintenance. You can use a spreadsheet, app, journal, or checklist to create a budget for yourself. Having it all laid out, will allow you to figure out where to make cuts, and to determine if you need to find a way to bring in more money. Talking to a financial planner/advisor can also be worth the investment. I am not suggesting that you hand over your money to someone, so that they can control it, rather learn the basics of how to take control of your financial well-being!

Love,
Me

Dear Single Woman,

When you are early, you give yourself the gift of time and peace. Running chronically late is not an act of self-love. Spending your day in a constant state of worry and feeling rushed, stresses out everyone and leaves you feeling tired and unproductive. Wake up 10 minutes earlier, and give yourself that sweet moment of silence before moving into the rest of your day. To have this experience later in the day, do any chores that you want done, before you sit down to rest. Then when you are finished, you can have a quiet evening and the time to relax and enjoy.

Love,
Me

Dear Single Woman,

I would love to tell you that everything works out, and it will all be all right. There are moments in our life, where that simply is not the truth, and I want to be truthful. There are things that can happen that make you question the truth, your worldviews, or how something so terrible can happen. Every bad feeling you have ever had will find its way to the surface, and you may want to sit in it like the last noodle that will not leave the bottom of the pot. After a while of scrubbing, the noodle gives up and succumbs to its fate. A little part sticks, and not even the scrubbiest of brushes can remove it. Time, water, and wear eventually release the last remnants of the clingy noodle. I know it is an odd metaphor, but we are like that, aren't we? We cling to the bottom and even when we move on, some part of our soul stays stuck in that moment in time. Some of you may even begin to identify yourself with that tragedy.

Here is an example of a Release Technique
Calling back the pieces:
Close your eyes, and take some deep breaths.
See yourself surrounded by the brightest, most beautiful light you have ever seen, and say:

"It is with love and forgiveness that I call back all of the missing pieces of my soul. I call it back from the past, present and future, to make myself whole again."

You may feel these pieces come back all at the same time or float in on a tiny silver thread. To me, they almost look like pieces of a mirror coming back into the puzzle of me.
Love,
Me

Dear Single Woman,

When you are ready to give up, do not. It is that simple; do not give up, unless, from your soul, you know that you are done. There is a difference between moving on from something that no longer brings you joy or has strayed too far from the goal and giving up. If you give up because you believe you cannot succeed, you are not good enough, or because someone put it into your head that the endeavor is not worthwhile, then you are laying to waste all of the energy that you already put into it. There are times when it is time to change your dream, not to stop dreaming, just change it. Suddenly, new energy flows in. It is ok to step away or give it a break, because it feels right. To leave a dream/goal out of fear, or lack of self-belief, could deprive the world of your greatness.

Love,
Me

Family, Friends, or Foes

Dear Single Woman,

Be careful who you listen to and who you choose to keep around you. The chaos that surrounds them will eventually surround you. The drama and games they play with others will slowly weave you into it. When you look at the people who are in your life, are they supportive of you and your pursuits? Are they available when you need an ear to listen or hands to help? Are they only available when something is going wrong in their life? Are they the first to gossip and the last to keep a secret? Do they feign caring, when you know, they only care about themselves? Do they make promises that they conveniently never keep? Do you find that your friends and family consistently expect you to give and compromise, but make you feel guilty, when you expect them to reciprocate? I know, it is a lot of questions, but these are ones that will help you weed out the healthy from the unhealthy.
The scary thing is that they are a reflection of your inner self. Are you breaking promises to yourself? Do you have a one sided relationship with yourself? Love yourself first. Then, fill your life with people who reflect that love. Always keep in mind that your life's journey will be much easier if you surround yourself with people that you love and love you in return.

Love,
Me

Dear Single Woman,

Surround yourself with people who are smarter, people whose opinions and mindsets may differ from yours. Learn from them, and listen with a quiet heart. Their opinions, though different, do not diminish yours, they enrich it. While politically you may lean in one direction, try tuning in to media that leans the other way. If you were raised in a particular spiritual belief, try learning about ones that are different.

Do not be afraid to change your mind or to grow from these experiences. If you are afraid that you will no longer know yourself, that is all right. We change ourselves all the time. We are a work in progress. Our wants, needs, aspirations, and dreams change and shift all the time, as we learn from those around us. You may find that by listening to others, it strengthens what you thought before, or adds some texture to your already beautiful picture. Whether you change or stay the same, be sure that the thoughts and beliefs you hold onto or let go of, is because that is what truly resonates with you, not because of pressure from the outside.

Love,
Me

Dear Single Woman,

Envy is a feeling that destroys everything that is important. Envy will eat away at your self-esteem, making you feel as if everyone else is better or better off. Remember, there is someone who is jealous of you. If you envy someone else's job, it can cause you to slack off where you are and ruin chances for upward movement. Comparing relationships is akin to injecting poison into yours. You have no idea what goes on behind closed doors. Focus on making your relationships the brightest and most loving possible. Your light cannot shine when you are worried about someone else's

Love,
Me

Dear Single Woman,

How is your day going? I am just asking in case you needed someone to. Oftentimes, the single world can be a cold and isolated place. Do not get me wrong; it can be liberating and freeing being single, but it can be a little lonely, as well. So how are you? Did you do something fun today? How was work? I miss seeing you and talking to you. You are a good friend, and we should talk more.

Reach out to your friends, and start up random conversations. Bring them closer, and make your world a little snugger.

Love,
Me

Dear Single Woman,

Your friends and family are more important than you can ever realize. They will call you on your crap and clean you up when you have stepped in it. They will ground you and bring clarity to the most complicated situations. They cannot, however, make your decisions for you and nor should they. They should be your sounding board, as you figure your own life out. As with any relationship, the ones with friends and family, can be quite complex. You may even need to take a break every now and then or break it off completely. The ones who stick around, through the highs and lows of your life are worth their weight in gold

Love,
Me

Dear Single Woman,

Saying goodbye is one of the hardest, but most necessary lessons of a person's life. I am not speaking of the goodbyes that really mean, "See you later." I am talking about the kind that ends a chapter of your life. The kind where you realize that turning back is no longer an option. This often involves grieving. It could be a loved one that passes away, but it could just as easily mark the end of a friendship. You may be excited for a new promotion, your own apartment, or moving across the country. However, the feeling of loss will find its way in there and how you handle that loss will determine the ease with which you live your newest chapter. Say your goodbyes, grieve your losses, and give yourself permission to experience joy again.

Love,
Me

Dear Single Woman,

Lessons from the snake:

Yes! Like the snake, as you grow, you will have to shed the skin of who you were. You will outgrow people and situations in your life. That is okay. If you live life right, you will always become a better and stronger version of yourself, not someone else. Patience will lead you to find what it is that you are waiting for, and sometimes you must show your teeth to get people to back off.

Love,
Me

Dear Single Woman,

Pay attention to what people say to your face about other people. Are they speaking kind words or criticism? Are they speaking honestly about someone else or are they excusing bad behavior? Are they saying the same things to their face that they would behind their backs? Pay attention, because you too are behind their backs some of the time. Be aware of the person who speaks badly of someone. Chances are if they speak ill of a person behind their back; they may be doing the same to you. Sharing concerns or frustrations is one thing, but gossiping and breaking confidence is another. It is perfectly acceptable to walk away from those kinds of conversations, by switching topics or physically making your exit.

Watch this within yourself. Be the person you want others to be to you. Venting is important; we all need to let off steam, just be sure that you are okay with it getting back to the person, or that you have shared this frustration with them already.

Love,
Me

Dear Single Woman,

Do not be afraid of the sharks. You or someone near you may see them coming. You know to stay away from those waters and where to move to be safe. It is not the big creatures who bare their teeth or posture and puff themselves up. Beware of those that move unseen, the smallest of creatures that can make you sick, or the ones who lack predictability. The people with those characteristics are the ones to be wary of and watched very carefully. They will strike when your guard is down, twist your words to cause pain, and take pleasure in watching you squirm. Once you are aware of them, they will move to an easier target.

Love,
Me

Dear Single Woman,

Do you feel unappreciated? That is normal and happens to everyone from time to time. Like love though, it must first begin with you. You have to show yourself gratitude, and then show appreciation for the people around you. When you have mastered that, you will begin to find yourself noticing the small blessings every day. You will be in such a state of gratitude, that the people, who had been neglecting you before, will no longer bother you. I know you may have been expecting me to say that they will start to show you appreciation back, but let us face it; people will not change until they are in a good emotional and mental space to do so. The bigger picture is that your need or craving for their appreciation will disappear, as it will not be very important any more. Your focus will be too busy on other things.

Love,
Me

Dear Single Woman,

When you are feeling low, reach out to your tribe, your circle, and your kindred spirits. Let them be a light of inspiration on your soul. They can be the brightest spot in your day. This is important to have in any aspect of your life, be it work, emotions, or financial. Those who are supportive of you without their ego becoming involved are worth their weight in gold! Find those people and connect, reconnect, communicate, and find joy in their light, as they find joy in yours.

Love,
Me

Dear Single Woman,

It does not matter how old you are, or what stage of life you are when this happens, but there may come a time when you find yourself living with family or roommates. Some words of advice:

- **Create** a space that is all your own. If you share a room, get a curtain or wall divider. A place for you to decompress and be alone will benefit all in the house.
- **Set** the ground rules of who is responsible for what. Then hold up your end of the bargain. If someone else is not, then say something in a healthy and non-confrontational way.
- **Do not** take out your outside anger on someone who has nothing to do with it. Vent about it, but also make sure they will not go blabbing. Just because you live with them does not oblige them to confidentiality.
- **Listen** to them. Make sure that they know that you value them as a friend or family member.
- **Have fun** together.
- If you do have a disagreement, **talk it out** and **don't** make it personal.

Sharing your space can be a wonderful experience, as long as, everyone is using healthy communication and does what they can to help. Each household looks different, and each member has something special they can bring to the table.

Love,
Me

Dear Single Woman,

There is a big difference between standing up for yourself and being hostile. Hostility is heavy and takes the power away from you and gives it to the person you are angry at. Standing up for yourself, takes the power back. You are going to be angry sometimes, but that does not mean you must thrash about like a toddler or become mean hearted towards someone else. Take a moment and look at the situation from their side, as it will help you to speak your mind in a way that they may understand. You may not always win the argument, but that is okay. Sometimes you must be an adult and agree to disagree.

Love,
Me

Lifestyle

Dear Single Woman,

You are the perfection in your job. You do not need to wait for the perfect job to find you or sit and complain about the one you have. All it takes is a shift of the attitude. No matter what job you have or what career path you have chosen, there will always be a down side. You will have bosses and coworkers who drive you nuts or throw you under the bus. There will be the customers who are never satisfied and find fault with everything. That does not mean it is a horrible job, rather, shift your focus to the people who appreciate you. Be the light in the darkness of your workspace. Ask to start a praise wall, where you boost each other up. Be the one who brings in the surprise coffee or tea for your work peeps. Focus on the client who loves what you do and ask for a testimonial. There are hundreds of ways to lighten up a bogged down environment, but adding to it with bitterness and anger, will only make you resent it more. The truth is that you will never move up and out unless people are able to see you bring something to the table. Start with a great attitude, and the rest will follow. If all else fails, be blessed by the paycheck and plan something fun for the end of your workweek!

Love,
Me

Dear Single Woman,

On politics: Develop your own mind. Party lines do not make a politician; they limit them, and you. Do they make policy based on who is paying them, or are they making policy based on what is best for their voters? Do their ethics allow them to maintain the integrity of their party? I hate to say this, but it is rare to find a politician who stays true to who they profess to be?

Why are you voting the way you do? Have you truly done the research? Is it to follow your friends and family? You have a voice, educate it, use it and make it powerful! Vote with knowledge and purpose and vote for someone who speaks and acts to your inner self. If you cannot find that person, perhaps you should run!

Love,
Me

Dear Single Woman,

Have I told you that every once and a while it is fantastic to be completely lazy? It is! Take a day, when you are off from work of course, and sleep until you wake up. That is delightful; to wake and know that if you want, you could roll over and fall right back to sleep. Have brunch or lunch and stay in your pjs. It is especially fun when you have the house to yourself. Spend the day however you like. My favorite way to spend the day is cuddled up with my dog, sipping coffee, and catching up on my DVR.

What does your perfect lazy day look like? Maybe you enjoy rising with the sun and reading a book or going for a walk. Then, maybe you want to follow it with the hobbies that always seem to get pushed to the side, ending with a popcorn and ice cream dinner. Put it in your schedule, and let the day unfold as you please. I am the type that works hard for long stretches at a time to get every bit of my work done, and then I hunker in for a long stretch of true relaxation. It is one of the best ways to bring balance into a busy life.

Enjoy!

Love,
Me

Dear Single Woman,

Know that a full life does not have to involve marriage and children. Oh, it can involve them; it just does not have to. We have been programmed to believe that in order to feel whole as a woman, you need to find a spouse and have children. Then when you do, you need grandchildren. The pressure never ends. Do not put pressure on yourself to fill roles that do not feel right for you. We live in a wonderful time where, in many parts of the world, women have the right to choose who they marry or if they marry. You can fill your time with friends, family, career, volunteer work, and hobbies. Then, if you do find someone, you will have so many interesting qualities to bring to the table. If you wait for your life to begin, it never will.

Love,
Me

Dear Single Woman,

There is no one right path to achieve anything. It is great to have role models and mentors, but theirs is a different path. Even my words here are not to be taken as gospel. Rather, take all of the wisdom and see what resonates and works for you. When you distill the truth down to their simplest forms, you will find that you vibrate either with it or against it. Then, make your choices accordingly.

Love,
Me

Dear Single Woman,

Being single can be exciting, liberating and amazing. However, there are many in society, who place a lot of "should's" on you. You should be married, you should have children, grandchildren and you should, should, should… it never stops. How about this, get married only if you find someone who makes your heart sing. Have children, because you feel that they are a treasure and will add to your life and you to theirs. Let your kids have or not have children, because it's right for them. Take the pressure off, and enjoy where you are in your life right now.

Love,
Me

Dear Single Woman,

There is no right way to live your life. You have many paths that lay before you, all of which are valid. Each path leads you to different choices and chances. There is a magical thread between fate and free will: Fate brings you to the fork in the road, while free will asks you to pick a side. It is easy to leave everything up to fate, but when you do, eventually you will stop moving forward. You must take the responsibility of your decisions, and understand that you have to work with the Universe/Fate/ Divine to make your life happen!

Love,
Me

Dear Single Woman,

Treat yourself like a vessel; what you fill your life with is who you become. A vessel filled with water becomes a water bottle, but if you fill it with wine, it is now a wine bottle. What you fill your mind, time and space with is what you will become. If you read about health, spend your time with healthy people, and make healthy choices; you are more likely to become a healthy person. This could be financial, physical, mental or spiritual health. Take time once a season, and reflect on how you are spending your time and what you do to fill your life. This time of reflection is especially important if you have been feeling off or unsatisfied with where you are in life. Some small changes could make a huge impact.

Love,
Me

Dear Single Woman,

It is ok to be "*That*" woman. Be that woman who says what you mean and means what you say. Be that woman who walks into work owning her bad self and knows she is going to rock it. Be that woman who has the shoulder to cry on and will use the other arm to defend her loved ones. (Figuratively speaking) Be that woman that does not care what others think or say (particularly about you), because you know who you are. Be that woman who can rock the sweats or a little black dress. Be that woman who can both buck the stereotype or embrace it. Be that woman who dares to dream and has the audacity to go for it. Be that woman who can cry the ugly tears or hold them back when there is business to take care of. Be the woman who is so full of integrity that the world cannot keep her down. Yeah, be "*That*" woman.

Love,
Me

Dear Single Woman,

Take the time to value hugs, and talking in person. Learn how to be alone with yourself and not feel lonely. Allow yourself to be a little less rushed and a little bit kinder to those around you. Every person is valuable; take time to learn the stories of those around you. I hope you realize how valuable you are. Learn the lessons of love and of community.

- If you find yourself lost, stop and get your bearings.
- If you find yourself alone, stop and learn to enjoy your own company.
- If you find yourself without work, stop and find a way to be useful, even if it is just for you.
- If you find yourself grieving, stop and let yourself grieve.

Then allow yourself to let the sun shine on you again. Your loved ones would want you to do just that!

Love,
Me

Dear Single Woman,

There are times when life will be hectic and crazy, and there will be times of silence and emptiness. Stop trying to rush through one to get to the other. Happiness and peace can be in both moments. It has to live within you. Take a few minutes of each day to breathe, center, and find your inner peace. Wear it like a warm sweater to get you through not only the day, but also enjoying the day.

- Take a quick walk
- Have a warm beverage
- Cuddle with your loved ones
- Write in a journal
- Meditate

You can do this anytime you need to bring your inner peace out to the surface. Remember, the "inside you" can also be your best friend.

Love,
Me

Dear Single Woman,

Take time to reevaluate your life goals and dreams. Do not get set in the world of *shoulds* and *have to's*. Those are dangerous and leave no room for growth and change. The person you are now has different goals and aspirations for yourself, than the person you were even just a year ago. Maybe your dreams have become more specific. Perhaps they have changed all together. It is perfectly fine to change your mind and let go of dreams that no longer serve your highest good. Allow for adjustments and live in amazement at where your journey takes you.

Love,
Me

Dear Single Woman,

Share your skills. Do not underestimate your gifts and talents; everyone has something to share. Be a mentor, supporter and guide for those who are rising up. Do not be threatened by their talent and gifts. As a teacher, I have learned that there will always be someone more advanced, even when they are newly emerging. The important thing to understand is that you will offer something unique. Different people will be attracted to your gifts and talents. You can have 20 hairdressers, and there will be clients who gravitate to each one for different reasons. You may find yourself moving from working with the crowd to becoming a teacher of teachers, healer of healers, trainer of athletes, mentor etc. There will always be clients who prefer to work with those who have years of experience. Be confident, strong, and ready to step into new incarnations of yourself and your career!

Love,
Me

Dear Single Woman,

When you open up to the power of your potential, everything begins to open up. Creativity flows, and the universe begins to present you with new opportunities. Start, by taking away the thoughts, "I can't," and my favorite, "Why do good things always happen to other people?" It took a slew of illnesses to strip me of everything I thought I wanted or had to do in my life. I let go of the "can't" and suddenly new books were written, speaking engagements offered, and limitations lifted in other areas of my life. This deep peace replaced the noise and clutter of my mind. I saw so clearly how I was standing in my own way. This happens with all of us. Even when people are wildly successful, they create new blocks to try to keep themselves where they are, but it stops them from moving to an even better place. It is like the viral videos of the dogs trying to figure out the passage blocked by plastic wrap. Some dogs are stuck and only look through whimpering and whining for help. Then, there are the dogs that plow right through it and get where they want to go. You could wait for help, or you could find a different way to get where you want to go (legally, safely and ethically, of course!)

Love,
Me

Dear Single Woman,

I would not want my life to be a fairytale. Most fairytales have a dark side, but we look at only the good side. In many fairytales, someone is hurt or mistreated. Someone close to you is lost forever; you live through curses and wishes. Only if you are lucky, will you happen upon the handsome/beautiful stranger who apparently is your soulmate. I do not want to rely on breadcrumbs to get me home, kiss up to a granter of wishes, or marry someone who fell in love with me before we ever spoke. Do not wish for your life to be a fairy tale. You rarely hear about the "ever afters;" you only hear about the "*happily* ever afters".

Love,
Me

Dear Single Woman,

There are times when we must relocate our balance. Find our center of being. Life sometimes throws our inner compass for a loop, and we lose all sense of who we are, what we want, and where we are going. When this happens, stop and take a break. It may be a long break, longer than you thought you needed. During this time, stay in, read books, and go for very long walks. Talk to yourself, and write it all out until your inspiration, energy and focus comes back. This time away will look different for everyone. It may be one long stretch, like a vacation or a new daily practice, while you continue to live the rest of your life. When this happens to me, it can be a stretch of months before everything clicks back into place. The trick is to not rush it, and just allow yourself to flow back into it.

Love,
Me

Dear Single Woman,

There are many types of journeys we will be called to take in our lifetime; the biggest one is life itself. Some are metaphorical and lead you to do some soul searching. You will travel to the innermost depths of yourself and probably come out with more questions than answers. Some are meant to take you to new places along with all of the wonder that lies within. Others will take you away from home for the first time, filling you with excitement and uncertainty. Sometimes you are led back home. Home is bittersweet, familiar and never quite, what you remembered. It seems a little smaller and as the people evolve, so does the place. Enjoy each and every journey you make. Take what you can, and leave behind you a trail of love: love of self, of people, and the Universe that contains us all.

Love,
Me

Dear Single Woman,

The next few letters are for my single women, who have been blessed with children or someone that they are taking care of long term. Just because one is single, does not mean that their life is freewheeling. We all have responsibilities, but we can find ourselves single again, or in charge of an entire household. This can happen at any age, and I would like to honor those who have taken on such an important role. Taking time for yourself, as I have said over and over, is vital. You have to take time FOR YOURSELF, be it 30 minutes or a weekend. Find trusted people that you can hire or are willing to help. When you recharge and rest, you will have more to give. It is simple and said by many professionals: friends, bosses, and family members. <u>You must make yourself a priority.</u> Even if you sneak an hour to yourself while everyone is asleep. Read, do yoga, listen to a podcast. Do something just for yourself, and do it regularly. Your body and mind will thank you for it, so will the people you take care of!

Love,
Me

Dear Single Woman,

If you are in the position of being a mother, as well as single, you have a huge responsibility to model self-love, self-care, and healthy relationships, not only for your sake, but also for the sake of your children. Ask yourself, "If my child was in a relationship, just like the one I am in, and came to me for advice, what would I tell them?" It can be difficult to see how toxic relationships (significant others, friends, family members, co-workers) can affect children. You pass on much more than genetics to your children. If you have body image issues, they are likely to, as well. If they hear you talk badly about yourself, they will likely mimic that, and worse, they may believe it of themselves. No parent is perfect, but the healthier you are in mind, body and spirit, you will find that your children will feel the good vibes coming off of you and want that for themselves. I do want to acknowledge that this is not the case for all children. Unfortunately, some children are just naturally tough on themselves or dealing with their own inner issues. However, your actions of modeling self-love, self-respect and fostering healthy relationships will, at the very least, set up a great foundation for them to carry into their adulthood.

Love,
Me

Dear Single Woman,

Take a play date with your kids, a day with as little stress as possible. It can be indoors or outdoors. Maybe you spend some fun money, or scavenger hunt for fun free activities. The idea is that being single and being a mom, means that everyone spends a lot of hectic time together. Emotions can run high and deep. The trick is to not over plan, and be ready for a change when a new mood strikes your children. They want a pillow fort and to eat dinner in there? Go for it! Want to cook together and eat under the sky? Yay. Someone makes a mess; make it bigger with them until you fall into a pile of giggles. Maybe it is a makeover day. Museums, bowling, the park, learn to sew, it does not matter as long as you are having stress free fun. Allow yourself to be playful, and let your inner child out to play, enjoy, and bask in the moment.
I would say the rules should be: phones away and no electronics, unless everyone is playing! While life can be stressful for a mom out on her own, it can be filled with fun and adventure, too.

Love,
Me

Dear Single Woman,

Let us flip the coin and say yes. Try new things, take a chance, and be a bit unexpected. Setting boundaries is very different from living in fear. A promotion comes up at work that you are qualified for, say yes. You may not get it, but it could put you on the radar for an even better promotion. Someone asks you out on a random date, and you find him or her smart, funny, and attractive… yes! You may find that they are not a great match, but if you do not try, you will never know for sure. Yes and no are very powerful words. One closes a door, and the other opens one. Used in the wrong way by overriding your needs and instincts, they could both potentially close doors for you. Be your truest authentic self by using these two words with confidence when they feel right.

Love,
Me

Dear Single Woman,

Do not be afraid to fail. Epic failures can ultimately lead to our biggest successes. We are moving away from a society that looks upon failure as a bad thing and moving into one of simple growth and learning. When you are little, you fail a million times, and everyone thinks it is adorable. The baby falls when learning to walk, and everyone claps. You try to say new words and mess it up thousands of times; that is adorable. If we continued to celebrate our missteps and mistakes with the same humor and adoration that we had as a child, we would be a whole lot farther, both as an individual and as a society.

Love,
Me

Dear Single Woman,

Sometimes sitting back and watching can be the best thing for you to do. Watch as the people go around you making their mistakes and living their lives. You know all too well that sometimes you just want a friend who will listen and not give their two cents. Alternatively, when you are about to make a mistake of your own, no amount of well-meaning advice will stop you. If there is drama that has nothing to do with you, step back and step away. Do not be the hero, because if it does not work, then they will turn their angst onto you. If you have trouble, sitting back and not doing anything, ask yourself why? Are you looking for the excitement, the drama or an ego boost? If so, there are healthier ways of achieving that. Become a volunteer. You will get the ego boost of being able to help, the excitement of meeting new people, and a dramatic change to your life!

Love,
Me

Dear Single Woman,

Foundations take time to build. All of those people that seem like an overnight success took years of building up, making connections, failing, trying again, before you see the finished result. The ones who do rise up very quickly into success also risk falling just as fast. The more patient you are building your life, the more solid and secure you will be, and the higher you rise. This happened to many of the child stars that had emotional breakdowns in their late teens and twenties. Their life looked glamorous to outsiders, but they were not prepared for the chaos, the ability of the public to turn on a dime, and the immense responsibility of their newfound wealth. Those very large burdens can lead to larger instability. You can build a mansion, but if you build it on sand, it will collapse. If you take your time and find beautiful solid ground, it could last for generations. Success is like that, too. So are relationships. Have you ever noticed how quickly-made friendships can fade in an instant, as well? Take your time, and enjoy the ride!

Love,
Me

Dear Single Woman,

If you have not heard it, I am proud of you. I am! You made it through many of life's difficulties and still keep going. When you felt like giving up and breaking down, you managed to work through it. Sure, it was difficult, but not impossible, and you proved it. You managed to let go of everything that you did not need any more, and you welcomed new opportunities. You realized that your tears did not mean that you were weak, no, those tears were a sign from your soul that life is changing. They washed away the old pain and left room for you to heal. Those words of anger did not mean that you were lashing out; rather you spoke your truth. When the truth was too painful, you offered words of apology, not because your truth changed, but because you cared for someone and the pain that was caused. I love the way you are able to admit when you are wrong and your flexibility to change your mind. I am proud of you for your strengths and your weaknesses. I admire you for your grace and empathy. I am in awe of your successes in all the ways it arrives, through the bumpy roads and the smooth ones, too.

Love,
Me

Dear Single Woman,

Be inspired by the many people and things around you. Be inspired by your family and friends. Be inspired by their toughness, resilience, and ability to laugh through it all. Be inspired by nature and by how we can experience both the vastness of the universe and find a universe within a single cell. Be inspired by the endless beauty and ability of our world to evolve and recreate itself repeatedly. Be inspired by our bodies and the way they can be pushed to the limits and to keep on going. Be inspired by how our minds contain the entire universe and yet, continue to expand. What inspires you? What moves you?

Love,
Me

Self-Love

Dear Single Woman,

Love takes many forms over your lifetime. Learn to notice and appreciate all of them. The love of yourself is the hardest and most important. Start early and recommit often. Love of family is both easy and complicated. We love them even when they hurt us. Simplify it and love them through their flaws, but do not allow them to put their past wounds on you. Set healthy boundaries. Friends are the family you choose, so choose wisely and recognize when to let go. Significant others are often the most confusing; do not confuse a lesson for a soulmate. Your children will be your greatest joy and greatest frustration. Enjoy both sides of that coin. Your pets are family; they, however, love you more than you love yourself. Love everyone with that same unconditional love that we all need and want.

Love,
Me

Dear Single Woman,

Listen to your body; it is talking to you every day. This is something to remind yourself often. Sleep, when you are tired. Eat when you are hungry. Dance when you feel like moving. Leave a person, place, or idea when your gut tells you that it is time to go. Take a leap of faith when your body gets all tingly with excitement, and stop when something feels very wrong. The phrase, "Your body is your temple," means that you should honor it, respect it, love it, and give thanks when it works well for you.

Love,
Me

Dear Single Woman,

Enjoy your alone time; enjoy your solitude. Being comfortable in quiet moments, will allow you to rest in a way that noise will not allow. No books, no radio, and no TV can tell you who you really are, the way silence can. Take a moment to picture and feel what it will look like. It may be uncomfortable at first, if you are used to the noise. Sometimes before I get started with my day, before the computer and phones go on, I take a silent snuggle with my dog. We look at each other and instead of mindless pets or scratches; I just enjoy our time together. Sometimes I sit with my cup of tea or coffee and look out of my window into the trees. Your quiet moments will look and feel different. Have a pen and paper to write down all of the random thoughts that come in, and then let them go. Maybe you will reflect upon the dreams of the night before. Learn to be alone in a way that is calming and brings you a sense of deep peace. You are awesome; why not take the time to know yourself better?

Love,
Me

Dear Single Woman,

You must be careful when choosing your role models. What you read on the internet and watch on television is so scripted that you cannot begin to live up to it. Your life is unique and unscripted. You are perfectly flawed and need no producer. Live your best life and stay true to yourself.

Fill in these blanks:
When I think of_____, I really admire_____ about them.

Then, ask yourself is it true, or just your perception of them based on editing, Photoshop, or simply the image they project. Even amongst friends and family, often you see only what they will allow you to see.

What do you admire about yourself? Are you allowing your unfiltered self to shine through?

When I think of myself, I really admire _____ about me.

(Write this one out on a piece of paper, and place it where you will see it often. This will remind you of something you like about yourself, and it will give you something positive on which to build.)

Love,
Me

Dear Single Woman,

Put no person on a pedestal. Pedestals are dangerous for the one who is up there and the one who puts them up there. Even those who have the appearance of goodness, the glow of eternal wisdom, have inner lives of which you are unaware. They have flaws that you cannot or will not see. It is unfair for you to adore someone based only on perceived perfection. Love them for the completely imperfect person they are.

Those types of relationships can be very painful when they end. When they do, it is usually because the goggles of perfection have suddenly come into focus for the first time. This can be too much for the other person to handle, and it eventually falls apart. Remember that being adored/idolized is different from being loved.

Love,
Me

Dear Single Woman,

Don't ignore the opposition, use it. Those that doubt you, who question your ability, can become your greatest asset. If used well, you very well could look back and say thank you for doubting me, I thoroughly enjoyed proving you wrong! Learn from the opposition, and let it fuel you. Let it fuel you to greater heights and massive success. Whatever success means to you let their negativity burn in you as a bright light. I relished proving others assumptions about me to be wrong; there were plenty. However, instead of allowing them the power to break me, I pushed back and pushed back more until they had nothing else to say. Go out there and kick some proverbial butt my friend!

Love,
Me

Dear Single Woman,

Be naked. No seriously, learn to be comfortable in your own skin. Appreciate it at every age. Love the flaws and the perfections. You do not want to look back and wish you had loved and appreciated what you had in your youth. No, instead love it now, and a year from now, and fifty years from now! Many women have spent their life wishing they were thinner, younger, prettier, and smoother. When in reality, they were already all of those things. They look back and think, "Oh how pretty I was," or "How thin I was," in that picture. You know what? At the time, they did not appreciate it. So that is your job, nay your quest, to love your vessel. You are beautiful, strong, and stunning right now. Look in the mirror with appreciation. If you cannot, then start small.

Fill in this sentence. (Tweak it if needed) Try this every day for a month or until it feels natural and your mind starts to shift.

"I love my_____; I adore how it is _____."

Love,
Me

Dear Single Woman,

Feed your spiritual body with regularity. There is no "right way" to do this. What feeds your soul one day, may not work the next, and you will need to change it up. Like so much of self-care, it is easy to get lost in the meaning. Some days, feeding your soul will look like a traditional meditation/prayer, with focus on breathing or journeying to the far reaches of the universe within. Other days, you will feed your soul by writing, painting, creating something beautiful or not so beautiful, as the case may be. It may occur naturally through your daily activities, like walking the dog or taking the time to clean a neglected corner of your home. You can choose to make it full of ritual or to take the rituals of daily life and turn them into a spiritual moment.

Love,
Me

Dear Single Woman,

You are amazing! You are! You are a miracle in human form, a string of events that stretch back past the dawn of time had to happen in just the right way for you to be here. You cannot be replicated and any copy would pale in comparison to you. Your thoughts, actions and life story have combined to make this incredible woman. Hold your head high, your back strong, and move through this world knowing that you are a work of art.

Whether you are full of sass and fire or sweet as sugar, it does not change your allure. Quiet and reserved or wagging a finger full of opinions; the world is better for having you in it. Your skin smooth as silk, or dimpled, wrinkled, stretched, scarred, all of it is beautiful. Let your heart feel that, and you can glow with that light that is all your own.

Just bask in that knowledge, the knowledge of your awesome uniqueness!

Love,
Me

Dear Single Woman,

Have you ever woken up to a delicious day? I mean one of those days that you are inexplicably content. Well, I am having one of those days: a crisp fall morning with a hot cup of tea, and I am ready for work early. I am sharing this with you in the hopes that you too, will find yourself in a delicious day.

When you do, take the time to savor the moment. Deep breathe, take note of your surroundings, so that you can have this in your memory bank for a positive thought in the future. Use it to help you meditate when you need to go to a good space.

Love,
Me

Dear Single Woman,

You are so loved, yet you may not even realize it. The millions of small things you do, can make a big difference to people around you. The smile you flash, door you hold, or dropped item you pick up, may be small unconscious acts, but they can make all the difference to someone having a bad day. Your impact is bigger than you will ever know and the love you show others, will always find its way back to you. Perhaps it will come from a stranger or friend you have not heard from in a long time. Maybe it will be given through a beautiful sunset or in the hug of a loved one, but love will find its way back to you.

You are loved by the people in your past and by those, you have yet to meet. Sure, there are people who leave and who do not realize your worth, and I am sorry for them. There will be days where you forget to love yourself and for that, I am sorry, too. There will be days where you are grumpy, angry and just feel unlovable. That is okay, because there is usually someone who loves you anyway, whether you feel like being it or not. No, not in the creepy way, don't be creepy. I mean that when you are sad, they want to wrap you in joy. When you are angry, they want to fight the world to make it better for you. Just know that you are loved.

Love,
Me

Dear Single Woman,

Your love is very valuable, your time precious, and your energy a treasure. Do not waste it. If someone wastes any of your love, time or energy, then it is time to rethink your connection with them. To stay connected out of guilt, obligation, or fear is simply a waste of everyone's everything. The other trap is convenience. Too many people stay with their significant others because it is "convenient" or "better than being alone." No, no it is not better than being alone. Being alone is far superior to being with someone you do not love, or with one who is not in love with you. Loneliness can hit sometimes, but never enough for you to go back to the awful relationships of your past. Remember the reasons you broke up and thank your lucky stars. Enjoy your time and love yourself enough to wait for someone worthy of your heart.

Love,
Me

Dear Single Woman,

The greatest love affair of your life will be with yourself. You will have days when you cannot stand yourself and when you want to break up with yourself. Then there will be days when you cannot get enough, when you see how beautiful you are and want yourself even more. Like every relationship, you must nurture it with patience, love and understanding. Be passionate and forgiving; love yourself the way you want someone else to love you.

Love,
Me

Dear Single Woman,

You are not a coin. Your value is not some arbitrary number assigned to you by society. Your value has nothing to do with how much money you may have in the bank. That amount just represents some time and energy you have spent. Instead, ask yourself; did I spend it well? Your value has nothing to do with your weight. Your weight just represents a combination of emotions, hormones, genetics, and calories. Instead, ask yourself, do I feed myself with love? Do I move my body with love? Do I feed the love or the stress? Your value has nothing to do with your age. Ask yourself, am I filling these years with joyful memories and loving people? Numbers only mean what people say they mean. We look at the number and know from childhood that that symbol represents one item plus another item. However, as a baby, that symbol has no meaning. As a baby, we know we want both of our loved ones arms holding us. We know that we want more of what we enjoy. As a child, there is only having and not having. There is no concept of how many. We are only in that moment of what is before us. Take time to see the world like that. What do I have now: time, space, joy, love, etc. Who am I now? Not what was I? What will I become? Instead ask, who am I now? Answering these questions honestly may help you shape your future.

Love,
Me

Dear Single Woman,

I know I may have already expressed these sentiments before, but they could use a little repeating. Living the single life is not about waiting for someone else to fill it. Single life is about filling it yourself. Fill it with glorious nights out, with friends, with family, with coworkers, and fill it with all the things that bring you joy. Have the wine, the chocolate, the gifts, the movies, and everything you think a partner will bring to you. Call yourself sexy and beautiful, dress up and look fantastic for yourself. Having a partner does not mean that they will do or say these things for you. They might, and woohoo if they do, that is great! However, if you practice giving yourself everything you want to experience in a relationship, then not only will you already feel fantastic (who isn't attracted to that?), but you will have so much to give to your partner and to expect in return.

Love,
Me

Dear Single Woman,

Words have power. Your words have power. Even when you feel as if no one listens to you, someone always is. Words can wrap you in comfort like the softest blanket or slice with deadly accuracy. Choose your words well, especially the ones you say to yourself. The unspoken dialogue that is heard by your soul can weigh heavily and recreate old narratives that no longer serve you. Speak words of love, encouragement, understanding, and forgiveness, not only to those around you, but also to yourself. When you are lost in thought, ask yourself, are you creating a world of wonder and excitement with those words and images, or are they heavy and full of negativity? If you find yourself in the latter, acknowledge them and release them allowing space for light to shine in.

Love,
Me

Dear Single Woman,

Have you ever looked at yourself and thought; "My life is a mess?" Then you are in fantastic company! Everyone around you has been there, is there, or will be there. Maybe it is finances, relationships, career, their hair, or their house, it does not matter. We have all been there. No matter how put together someone around you seems, they have their own version of mess going on. Do not compare messes, or even think there is anything wrong with it. As we take time to clean ourselves, that is where transformation, learning, and evolution take place. Sometimes it will get worse before it gets better, and that is ok. We are all a glorious work in progress! Embrace your messes, and rejoice in your evolutions.

Love,
Me

Dear Single Woman,

There are so many people and places offering you the easy way out. Usually in 3-10 easy steps, but rarely is true transformation easy. Think of the butterfly, they must let go of their old form, of who they thought they were to become a completely new creature. Does the caterpillar know its future, when it creates the cocoon or does it go with the flow and follow its instincts until suddenly it is newly evolved? Perhaps that is the easiness, not in steps, but in following our inner voice and pulling until we are in a future that we never could have seen for ourselves. It takes an immense amount of energy, mixed with trust, that all will be as it should when we come out of hiding and resting. Take your time, have a little faith, work your butt off, and let go of everything the world told you, you were; so that you can become everything you were meant to be.

Love,
Me

Dear Single Woman,

How often do you talk to yourself? Moreover, how often do you listen to yourself? Make it a daily practice. It does not matter how or where, just that you stop and listen to your mind, body, spirit, and emotions on a daily basis. Loving yourself is the same as loving someone else; it takes time, energy, and lives in the small gestures. Grand gestures are nice and all, but that is not what makes me feel the love from someone. It is in how they look at me, how they know when I need a cup of tea or a reassuring hand on my back. It is the same with how we treat ourselves. Learn when you need to rest, eat, play and sleep. Look at yourself with appreciation, and give yourself that pat on the back. You are important to all of the people who rely on you; you need to be that important to yourself.

Love,
Me

Dear Single Woman,

A Goddess dims her light for no one. She makes no apologies for her greatness. Each step she takes, makes the world all the brighter for her being in it. She moves with purpose and confidence. If someone shames you for your glow, shine brighter. If there are those who are threatened by you, it is because they have not yet stepped into their power. Share your light, shine it and help others to rise.

Love,
Me

Dear Single Woman,

We are taught to look for flaws and to hunt out imperfections. It is perfectly fine to look around at your life and be, "My life is damn near perfect right now!" Maybe it is just in that moment, or maybe your hard work has paid off. Sometimes, you can sit back and enjoy the fruits of your labor. Do not wait for the other shoe to drop, do not be all; this is too good to be true. Sure, everything can use some amount of improvement, but sometimes, life is pretty good as it is. Enjoy the moment.

Love,
Me

Dear Single Woman,

There is a power in saying, "No," Big NO's little no's. It is you setting up boundaries. "No," can feel very uncomfortable, as we are programmed to say yes. From a young age, people have instructed us to hug so and so, and because we aim to please we go forth and hug. We eat foods that we do not like, because we do not want the cook to feel bad. We go out with our friends when we want to stay home, or stay home because someone we love does not want to go out. Sometimes, we should explore life, and we should push outside of our comfort zones. Compromise is needed when you live in and amongst society, compromise must happen for everyone's benefit. That being said, self-care is important. Listening to your body, mind, and spirit is important; it will help you set up those "healthy" boundaries. If you really do not want to go hang out with your peeps, because you need a night in, then say no or even better, "not now." Not now is a fantastic alternative that leaves some flexibility. In the end, everyone can benefit from the occasional "no," so go for it and try it.

Love,
Me

Dear Single Woman,

When I sit here thinking about the word Love. The song of the same title from Nat King Cole pops into my head. Go look up the lyrics and apply them to yourself. I know I have written on self-love before, but it is so important, it bears repeating. You are worthy of your time, your effort, and your investment. However, remember there are levels of self-love. Are you slacking off? Are you just checking off the self-love to do list? Sleep - check Eat – check, do some affirmations - check Meditate - check exercise, and eat right - check, check. We see couples doing that all the time. They love by rote, but not by feeling. Love yourself with passion every day. That passion will start to light up rooms and inspire others. You will have much more to give to other people. We all have to work on that basic checklist, but we should go above and beyond, every once and awhile. Surprise ourselves with fresh flowers, our favorite dinner, a night out. We should feel our bodies and souls call and answer. Sometimes a simple meditation is not enough, perhaps a full week off the grid at a retreat or a place where we can hear the birds sing and see the stars at night. Maybe it is going home, reconnecting with loved ones, and finding that younger self to re-inspire joy. However, you choose to love yourself, be more than a checklist, unless you are passionate about checklists, then okay, be a check list.

Love,
Me

Dear Single Woman,

You are this amazing miracle. Please let that sink in. Everything that has come together, to make you who you are, can never be fully re-created. Your heart, mind, and body are strong, yet fragile. They are yours and need to be well cared for. Place your future into your own very capable hands to mold and shape into everything that you have ever wanted. When you look around and see that you are not yet where you want to be, stop and say that word "yet." If you choose, you can make changes that will bring you there. Savor the "in between" moments: those small moments that happen while you are busy looking to your future. You will find your opportunities, chances, and choices in those moments. You will also find memories, friendships, help, release, and a million other things that will make your life whole and full. Being single, does not define you, but how you live, celebrate, strive, and connect with others, does. If you find the people, who have your back and love you the way you should love yourself, you will never be lonely. Date because you want to, not because you have to. If you should find someone, remember to honor each other's individuality so that you can be stronger together. Love yourself unconditionally, and remember the miracle that you are.

Love,
Me

Notes

www.ingramcontent.com/pod-product-compliance
Lightning Source LLC
Chambersburg PA
CBHW051653040426
42446CB00009B/1112